KEATON CAMPBELL

The Poverty Killer: Live Life on Your Terms

This book was professionally typeset on Reedsy.
Find out more at reedsy.com

Contents

Chapter 1: The Road to Financial Freedom

Have you ever dreamed of a life where you don't have to worry about money? Where you can pursue your passions and spend time with the people you love without the constant stress of bills and debt? This is the promise of financial freedom, a state of being where you have enough money to live the life you want on your terms.

For many of us, the road to financial freedom can seem daunting or even impossible. We may feel trapped by our jobs, burdened by student loans, or overwhelmed by the rising costs of housing and healthcare. But the truth is that financial freedom is within reach for anyone who is willing to work for it.

To begin the journey towards financial freedom, we must first understand what it means. Financial freedom is not about being rich or having a certain amount of money in the bank. It's about having the resources and flexibility to live the life you want without worrying about money. It means having enough savings to cover emergencies, investing wisely for the future, and living within your means.

Achieving financial freedom requires a mindset shift. We must move away from the idea that money equals success or happiness and instead focus on building a sustainable lifestyle that supports our goals and values. This means learning how to budget effectively, avoiding debt, and investing in our future.

The good news is that there are many resources available to help us on this journey. From financial advisors to online courses and books, there is no shortage of information and support for those who are committed to achieving financial freedom.

But perhaps the most important step we can take towards financial freedom is to simply start. Whether it's opening a savings account, paying off debt, or investing in our retirement, every small step we take brings us closer to the life we want.

In the chapters ahead, we'll explore the principles and strategies that can help you achieve financial freedom. From understanding the power of compound interest to building a diversified investment portfolio, we'll provide you with the tools and knowledge you need to take control of your financial future. So, are you ready to take the first step towards financial freedom? Let's begin.

Chapter 2: Being Smart with Your Money

I t's a common misconception that having a lot of money automatically translates to financial freedom. However, as many professional athletes and lottery winners have learned the hard way, being careless with your money can lead to financial ruin.

In fact, a staggering 60% of all professional sports players end up broke within just five years of retiring. This is often due to a combination of factors, including overspending, poor financial advice, and lack of financial literacy. Similarly, lottery winners who are ignorant with their newfound wealth often end up worse off than before they won.

So, what can we learn from these cautionary tales? The key to achieving and maintaining financial freedom is being smart with our money. This means having a solid understanding of personal finance and making informed decisions about how we earn, spend, and invest our money.

One of the first steps to being smart with our money is creating and sticking to a budget. This means tracking our income and expenses, setting financial goals, and prioritizing our spending accordingly. It may also mean making sacrifices in the short-term in order to achieve our long-term goals.

Another important aspect of being smart with our money is avoiding debt whenever possible. While some types of debt, such as a mortgage or student loans, may be necessary, high-interest credit card debt can quickly spiral out of control. By living within our means and avoiding unnecessary expenses, we can minimize our reliance on debt and avoid the stress and financial burden that comes with it.

Investing wisely is also crucial to achieving financial freedom. This means diversifying our portfolio and avoiding risky investments that could lead to significant losses. By taking a long-term approach and seeking professional financial advice, we can make informed decisions about how to grow our wealth and ensure a secure financial future.

Ultimately, being smart with our money is about taking control of our finances and making informed decisions about how we earn, spend, and invest our money. By avoiding the pitfalls of overspending, debt, and poor investment decisions, we can build a strong financial foundation and achieve the freedom to live the life we want on our own terms.

Chapter 3: The Power of a Smart Budget

W hen it comes to achieving financial freedom, a smart budget is an essential tool. Not only does it help you to track your spending, but it also shows you exactly where your money is coming from and where it's going.

By creating a budget, you can identify your sources of income, your monthly expenses, and any debts you may have. This allows you to gain a clear picture of your financial situation and make informed decisions about how to manage your money.

One of the biggest benefits of having a smart budget is that it allows you to see exactly how much money you have coming in and going out each month. This knowledge can be powerful, as it helps you to prioritize your spending and make sure you're not overspending on unnecessary expenses.

For example, you may find that you're spending too much money on eating out or on subscription services that you rarely use. By cutting back on these expenses, you can free up more money to put towards your financial goals, such as paying off debt or building up savings.

In addition, a smart budget can help you to identify cash flowing assets, which are assets that generate income over time. Unlike a car or a house, which are not considered assets, cash flowing assets can help you to build wealth and achieve financial freedom.

Examples of cash flowing assets include rental properties, stocks, and bonds. By including these assets in your budget and investing in them wisely, you can generate passive income and increase your net worth over time.

In summary, a smart budget is a powerful tool that can help you to take control of your finances and achieve financial freedom. By understanding where your money is coming from and going, you can make informed decisions about how to manage your money, prioritize your spending, and build wealth over time.

Chapter 4: The Importance of Cash Flowing Assets

When it comes to achieving financial freedom, one of the most important concepts to understand is the difference between assets and liabilities. Many people mistakenly believe that their home or their job is an asset, but in reality, these are not considered assets in the financial sense.

An asset is something that generates income and has the potential to increase in value over time. Examples of assets include rental properties, businesses, stocks, bonds, and precious metals such as gold and silver. These are all forms of wealth that can provide cash flow and long-term value.

On the other hand, a liability is something that costs money and does not generate income. Examples of liabilities include your primary residence, car loans, credit card debt, and personal loans. These are all forms of debt that can eat away at your income and limit your ability to build wealth over time.

One of the best examples of a cash flowing asset is a rental property. When you invest in a rental property, you have the potential to generate passive income through rent payments. In addition, the property itself can increase in value over time, providing you with long-term wealth.

Another example of a cash flowing asset is a business. When you own a successful business, you have the potential to generate income through sales and profits. A successful business can also increase in value over time, providing you with long-term wealth.

In contrast, your primary residence is not considered a cash flowing asset. While it may increase in value over time, it does not generate income and can actually be a liability if you have a mortgage to pay. Similarly, working a job is not considered a cash flowing asset, as it only provides income while you are actively working.

In summary, understanding the difference between assets and liabilities is key to achieving financial freedom. By investing in cash flowing assets such as rental properties, businesses, and precious metals, you can generate passive income and build long-term wealth. This can help you to achieve financial independence and create a more secure future for yourself and your family.

Chapter 5: Leveraging Debt to Multiply Your Wealth

D ebt is often viewed as a negative thing, but when used strategically, it can actually be a powerful tool for multiplying your wealth. By leveraging debt, you can take a small amount of money and turn it into a much larger sum over time.

One of the most common ways to leverage debt is through real estate investing. For example, if you have $50,000 to invest, you could use that money to buy one property outright. However, if you instead put a $25,000 down payment on two properties, you could potentially double your cash flow and increase your potential for long-term wealth.

The key to successful real estate investing is to carefully analyze the potential return on investment for each property and ensure that the cash flow generated by the properties is greater than the cost of the debt used to finance them. This requires a thorough understanding of the real estate market and the ability to identify undervalued properties with strong income potential.

Another way to leverage debt is through asset-based lending, such as using gold or other precious metals as collateral for a loan. For example, if you own $10,000 worth of gold, you may be able to borrow up to

80% of the value of the gold through a collateral loan. This allows you to access funds without actually selling your gold, and you can use the borrowed money to invest in other cash flowing assets or opportunities.

Of course, it's important to use debt carefully and wisely. Taking on too much debt can be risky and lead to financial instability. It's important to have a solid plan in place and to carefully consider the potential risks and rewards before using debt to leverage your investments.

In summary, leveraging debt can be a powerful tool for multiplying your wealth and achieving financial freedom. By carefully analyzing potential investments and using debt wisely, you can take a small amount of money and turn it into a much larger sum over time. However, it's important to be mindful of the risks involved and to have a solid plan in place before taking on debt to finance your investments.

Chapter 6: Tax Strategies for Maximizing Your Wealth

Taxes are a fact of life, but there are strategies you can use to legally minimize the amount of taxes you pay and keep more of your hard-earned money. Understanding the different types of employees and how they are taxed is an important first step in developing a tax strategy that works for you.

There are four types of employees: self-employed, traditional employees, big business owners with 500 or more employees, and investors. Traditional employees, such as those who work for a company, typically pay the highest taxes. Self-employed individuals also pay a significant amount of taxes, as they are responsible for paying both the employee and employer portions of Social Security and Medicare taxes.

Big business owners with 500 or more employees often have access to a range of tax breaks and incentives, such as research and development tax credits and tax deductions for employee benefits. However, these tax breaks are often not available to smaller businesses or self-employed individuals.

Investors, on the other hand, have access to a variety of tax strategies that can help them legally minimize their tax liability. One such strategy is debt leveraging. By taking on debt to invest in income-producing assets, investors can use the interest payments on the debt to offset their taxable income.

Another tax strategy for investors is the 1031 exchange. This allows investors to defer paying taxes on the sale of an investment property by reinvesting the proceeds in a similar property within a certain timeframe. This can be a powerful tool for growing your wealth over time while minimizing your tax liability.

It's important to work with a tax professional who can help you navigate the complexities of the tax code and develop a customized tax strategy that meets your unique needs and goals. By taking advantage of the various tax strategies available to you, you can legally minimize your tax liability and keep more of your hard-earned money in your pocket.

In summary, taxes are a significant expense for many individuals and businesses. By understanding the different types of employees and the tax strategies available to investors, you can develop a customized tax strategy that helps you legally minimize your tax liability and maximize your wealth over time. Working with a tax professional can help you navigate the complexities of the tax code and ensure that you are taking advantage of all available tax breaks and incentives.

Chapter 7: Types of Income and Tax Savings

I ncome is the lifeblood of any financial strategy, but not all income is created equal. Understanding the different types of income and how they are taxed is essential for maximizing your wealth and minimizing your tax liability.

One type of income is passive income, which is earned through rental properties, dividend-paying stocks, and other investments. Passive income is generally tax-free or subject to a lower tax rate than other forms of income, making it an attractive source of income for investors.

Another way to save money on taxes is to set up a limited liability company (LLC) or an S-corporation. These business structures allow business owners to pay themselves a smaller salary while running distributions into the company. By doing this, you can reduce your tax liability by paying self-employment tax only on your salary, rather than the entire income of the business.

For example, let's say you own a small business that earns $100,000 in profits each year. If you run the profits as distributions, it stays in the company, and you only pay self-employment tax on your small salary. This can result in significant tax savings over time.

Additionally, LLCs and S-corporations offer liability protection for business owners, making them a popular choice for small business owners and entrepreneurs.

It's important to work with a tax professional or financial advisor to determine which business structure is right for you and to ensure that you are complying with all tax laws and regulations. Setting up the right business structure can help you save money on taxes and protect your personal assets from business liabilities.

In summary, understanding the different types of income and how they are taxed is essential for maximizing your wealth and minimizing your tax liability. Passive income, such as rental income and dividend-paying stocks, can be a tax-free source of income for investors. Setting up an LLC or S-corporation can also help you save money on taxes by running profits as distributions and paying yourself a smaller salary. Working with a tax professional or financial advisor can help you navigate the complexities of tax law and ensure that you are making the most of available tax-saving strategies.

Chapter 8: Understanding Portfolio Income and Taxes

Portfolio income is a type of income that comes from investments, such as stocks, bonds, and mutual funds. Unlike passive income, which is earned through rental properties and other investments, portfolio income is generated through buying and selling assets in the financial markets.

Portfolio income can be taxed differently depending on how long the assets are held and whether they are sold for a profit or a loss. If an asset is held for less than one year and sold for a profit, it is considered a short-term capital gain and is taxed at ordinary income tax rates. If an asset is held for more than one year and sold for a profit, it is considered a long-term capital gain and is taxed at a lower rate than short-term gains.

On the other hand, if an asset is sold for a loss, the loss can be used to offset capital gains and up to $3,000 of ordinary income each year. Any remaining losses can be carried forward to future tax years.

It's important to note that portfolio income is subject to capital gains taxes, which can be complex and vary depending on your income level and the types of investments you hold. Working with a financial advisor or tax professional can help you navigate these complexities and develop a tax-efficient investment strategy.

One way to minimize your tax liability on portfolio income is through tax-loss harvesting, which involves selling investments that have decreased in value to offset gains and reduce your overall tax bill. Another strategy is to hold investments in tax-advantaged accounts, such as an individual retirement account (IRA) or a 401(k), which can defer or eliminate taxes on portfolio income until the funds are withdrawn in retirement.

In summary, portfolio income is a type of income generated through buying and selling investments, such as stocks, bonds, and mutual funds. It is subject to capital gains taxes, which can be complex and vary depending on the type of investment and how long it is held. Working with a financial advisor or tax professional can help you develop a tax-efficient investment strategy and navigate the complexities of capital gains taxes.

Chapter 9: The Downsides of Earned Income

E arned income is the most common type of income for most people. It is income that is earned through work, whether it's through a salary, hourly wages, or commissions. Unfortunately, earned income is also the most highly taxed type of income and is the least beneficial to the recipient compared to other types of income.

Earned income is subject to both federal and state income taxes, as well as payroll taxes, which include Social Security and Medicare taxes. In some cases, the total tax rate on earned income can reach 50% or more, depending on the individual's income level.

In addition to the high tax rate, earned income has other disadvantages. For one, it is dependent on the individual's ability to work, which can be impacted by age, health, and other factors. Earned income is also limited by the number of hours that can be worked in a day or week, which can limit the earning potential.

Another disadvantage of earned income is that it is not passive, meaning it requires ongoing effort to continue earning. This can lead to burnout, stress, and a lack of work-life balance, which can ultimately impact the individual's overall quality of life.

Despite these downsides, earned income is still a necessary part of most people's lives. However, it's important to recognize the limitations of earned income and work towards generating other types of income, such as passive income or portfolio income. By diversifying your sources of income, you can reduce your reliance on earned income and create a more stable financial future for yourself.

In conclusion, earned income is the most common type of income for most people, but it is also the most highly taxed and least beneficial type of income. By recognizing the downsides of earned income and working towards generating other types of income, you can reduce your reliance on earned income and create a more stable financial future for yourself.

Chapter 10:Diversified protection

I n today's world, it's not enough to rely on just one source of income. In order to truly be successful and financially independent, one must look for opportunities to make money in various areas.

Diversifying your portfolio is key to achieving financial freedom. As well as keeping it safe against wealth attacks. You should allocate your assets across different asset classes, such as stocks, bonds, precious metals, real estate, and cash flow assets. A well-diversified portfolio can help reduce your overall investment risk. Each one of these categories should be diversified as well.

Examples:
Stocks: you should have different types of stocks and in different industries,
Precious Metals: Gold, Silver, Platinum, Palladium.

by doing this you make the safety of your wealth sky rocket.

A commonly recommended asset allocation strategy is to allocate 20% of your portfolio to stocks and bonds, 10% to cash, 20% to precious metals and jewelry, 10% to personal equity (such as your own business or intellectual property), and 20% to real estate. The remaining 20% should be allocated to cash flow assets, such as rental properties, dividend-paying stocks, or a small business.

However, it's important to note that this asset allocation strategy may not be suitable for everyone, as everyone's financial goals and risk tolerance may differ. It's important to do your own research and consult with a financial advisor before making any investment decisions.

By diversifying your portfolio and investing in various asset classes, you can increase your chances of success and achieve financial freedom. Remember, always be on the lookout for new opportunities to make money and grow your wealth.

Chapter 11:The Abundance of Wealth and the Power of Hard Work

Many people believe that only a select few have the ability to become rich and financially free. However, the reality is that there is an abundance of wealth in the world, and anyone can achieve financial success with the right mindset and approach.

The problem is not that there is a lack of money, but rather a lack of people who are willing to put in the hard work and consistency required to achieve their financial goals. Many individuals are content with their current financial situation and do not see the need to put in the effort to improve it. However, those who are determined to succeed and are willing to work hard will find that there are countless opportunities to make money.

Success is not just about luck or being in the right place at the right time. It is about having a clear vision of what you want to achieve and being willing to put in the time and effort to make it happen. Whether it is starting a business, investing in stocks, or pursuing real estate, there are countless ways to build wealth and achieve financial freedom.

However, it is important to understand that success will not happen overnight. It requires consistent effort, focus, and dedication. It is easy to become discouraged when faced with setbacks or challenges, but those who persevere and stay committed to their goals will eventually reap the rewards of their hard work.

In conclusion, the key to achieving financial success is to adopt a mindset of abundance and understand that there are countless opportunities to make money in the world. By putting in the hard work and staying focused on your goals, you too can achieve financial freedom and live the life you have always dreamed of.

Chapter 12: Go Get It!!

Congratulations, you have made it to the final chapter of this book. I hope that by now you have gained the knowledge and skills necessary to achieve financial freedom. But knowledge alone is not enough, you must also have the determination and motivation to take action.

In this final chapter, I want to remind you that nothing is impossible. You can achieve anything you set your mind to, including becoming financially independent. It may not happen overnight, but with hard work and persistence, you can make it a reality.

Remember that success is not just about making money, it's about achieving your dreams and living the life you want. It's about creating a legacy for yourself and your loved ones. It's about being able to give back to your community and help those in need.

Don't let fear or doubt hold you back. Believe in yourself and your abilities. Take calculated risks and be willing to step out of your comfort zone. Don't be afraid to fail, because failure is just an opportunity to learn and grow.

Surround yourself with people who support and encourage your goals.

Seek out mentors and role models who have achieved financial success and learn from their experiences.

Most importantly, remember that wealth is not just about money. It's about having a rich and fulfilling life. Don't sacrifice your health, relationships, or values in pursuit of wealth. Stay true to yourself and what matters most to you.

In conclusion, I want to leave you with this final thought: you have the power to create the life you want. It may not be easy, but it's worth it. So go out there, chase your dreams, and become the master of your own destiny.